Sophie's World
The Greek Philosophers

JOSTEIN GAARDER

A Phoenix paperback

First published in Great Britain by Phoenix House in 1995

This abridged edition published in 1996 by Phoenix
a division of Orion Books Ltd
Orion House, 5 Upper St Martin's Lane, London WC2H 9EA

This abridged edition, published in 1996 by Phoenix, contains extracts
from the chapters *The Natural Philosophers, Democritus, Fate, Socrates,
Athens, Plato, The Major's Cabin, Aristotle,* from *Sophie's World*

ISBN 1 85799 587 2

Typeset by Selwood Systems, Midsomer Norton
Printed in Great Britain by Clays Ltd, St Ives plc.

CONTENTS

The Natural Philosophers

The earliest Greek philosophers are sometimes called *natural philosophers* because they were mainly concerned with the natural world and its processes.

Nowadays a lot of people imagine that at some time something must have come from nothing. This idea was not so widespread among the Greeks. For one reason or another, they assumed that 'something' had always existed.

How everything could come from nothing was therefore not the all-important question. On the other hand the Greeks marveled at how live fish could come from water, and huge trees and brilliantly colored flowers could come from the dead earth. Not to mention how a baby could come from its mother's womb!

The philosophers observed with their own eyes that nature was in a constant state of transformation. But how could such transformations occur?

How could something change from being substance to being a living thing, for example?

All the earliest philosophers shared the belief that there had to be a certain basic substance at the root of all change. How they arrived at this idea is hard to say. We only know that the notion gradually evolved that there must be a basic substance that was the hidden cause of all changes in nature.

There had to be 'something' that all things came from and returned to.

For us, the most interesting part is actually not what solutions these earliest philosophers arrived at, but which questions they asked and what type of answer they were looking for. We are more interested in how they thought than in exactly what they thought.

We know that they posed questions relating to the transformations they could observe in the physical world. They were looking for the underlying laws of nature. They wanted to understand what was happening around them without having to turn to the ancient myths. And most important, they wanted to understand the actual processes by studying nature itself. This was quite different from explaining thunder and lightning or winter and spring by telling stories about the gods.

So philosophy gradually liberated itself from religion. We could say that the natural philosophers took the first step in the direction of scientific reasoning, thereby becoming the precursors of what was to become science.

Only fragments have survived of what the natural philosophers said and wrote. What little we know is found in the writings of Aristotle, who lived two centuries later. He refers only to the conclusions the philosophers reached. So we do not always know by what paths they reached these conclusions. But what we do know enables us to establish that the earliest Greek philosophers' project concerned the question of a basic constituent substance and the changes in nature.

Three Philosophers from Miletus

The first philosopher we know of is *Thales,* who came from Miletus, a Greek colony in Asia Minor. He traveled in many countries, including Egypt, where he is said to have calculated the height of a pyramid by measuring its shadow at the precise moment when the length of his own shadow was equal to his height. He is also said to have accurately predicted a solar eclipse in the year 585 B.C.

Thales thought that the source of all things was water. We do not know exactly what he meant by that, he may have believed that all life originated from water – and that all life returns to water again when it dissolves.

During his travels in Egypt he must have observed how the crops began to grow as soon as the floods of the Nile receded from the land areas in the Nile Delta. Perhaps he also noticed that frogs and worms appeared wherever it had just been raining.

It is likely that Thales thought about the way water turns to ice or vapor – and then turns back into water again.

Thales is also supposed to have said that 'all things are full of gods.' What he meant by that we can only surmise. Perhaps, seeing how the black earth was the source of everything from flowers and crops to insects and cockroaches, he imagined that the earth was filled with tiny invisible 'life-germs.' One thing is certain—he was not talking about Homer's gods.

The next philosopher we hear of is *Anaximander,* who also lived in Miletus at about the same time as Thales. He thought that our world was only one of a myriad of worlds that evolve and dissolve in something he called the boundless. It is not so easy to explain what he meant by the boundless, but it seems clear that he was not thinking of a known substance in the way that Thales had envisaged. Perhaps he meant that the substance which is the source of all things had to be something other than the things created. Because all created things are limited, that which comes before and after them must be 'boundless.' It is clear that this basic stuff could not be anything as ordinary as water.

A third philosopher from Miletus was *Anaximenes* (c. 570–526 B.C.). He thought that the source of all things must be 'air' or 'vapor.' Anaximenes was of course familiar with Thales' theory of water. But where does water come from? Anaximenes thought that water was condensed air. We observe that when it rains, water is pressed from the air. When water is pressed even more, it becomes earth, he thought. He may have seen how earth and sand were pressed out of melting ice. He also thought that fire was rarefied air. According to Anaximenes, air was therefore the origin of earth, water, and fire.

It is not a far cry from water to the fruit of the earth. Perhaps Anaximenes thought that earth, air, and fire were all necessary to the creation of life, but that the source of all things was air or vapor. So, like Thales, he thought that there must be an underlying substance that is the source of all natural change.

Nothing Can Come from Nothing

These three Milesian philosophers all believed in the existence of a single basic substance as the source of all things. But how could one substance suddenly change into something else? We can call this the *problem of change*.

From about 500 B.C., there was a group of philosophers in the Greek colony of Elea in Southern Italy. These 'Eleatics' were interested in this question.

The most important of these philosophers was *Parmenides* (c. 540–480 B.C.). Parmenides thought that everything that exists had always existed. This idea was not alien to the Greeks. They took it more or less for granted that everything that existed in the world was everlasting. Nothing can come out of nothing, thought Parmenides. And nothing that exists can become nothing.

But Parmenides took the idea further. He thought that there was no such thing as actual change. Nothing could become anything other than it was.

Parmenides realized, of course, that nature is in a constant state of flux. He perceived with his senses that things changed. But he could not equate this with what his reason told him. When forced to choose between relying either on his senses or his reason, he chose reason.

You know the expression 'I'll believe it when I see it.' But Parmenides didn't even believe things when he saw them. He believed that our senses give us an incorrect picture of the world, a picture that does not tally with our reason. As a philosopher, he saw it as his task to expose all forms of perceptual illusion.

This unshakable faith in human reason is called *ration-*

alism. A rationalist is someone who believes that human reason is the primary source of our knowledge of the world.

All Things Flow

A contemporary of Parmenides was *Heraclitus* (c. 540–480 B.C.), who was from Ephesus in Asia Minor. He thought that constant change, or flow, was in fact the most basic characteristic of nature. We could perhaps say that Heraclitus had more faith in what he could perceive than Parmenides did.

'Everything flows,' said Heraclitus. Everything is in constant flux and movement, nothing is abiding. Therefore we 'cannot step twice into the same river.' When I step into the river for the second time, neither I nor the river are the same.

Heraclitus pointed out that the world is characterized by opposites. If we were never ill, we would not know what it was to be well. If we never knew hunger, we would take no pleasure in being full. If there were never any war, we would not appreciate peace. And if there were no winter, we would never see the spring.

Both good and bad have their inevitable place in the order of things, Heraclitus believed. Without this constant interplay of opposites the world would cease to exist.

'God is day and night, winter and summer, war and peace, hunger and satiety,' he said. He used the term 'God,' but he was clearly not referring to the gods of the mythology. To Heraclitus, God – or the Deity – was something that embraced the whole world. Indeed, God can be seen most clearly in the constant transformations and contrasts of nature.

Instead of the term 'God,' Heraclitus often used the Greek word *logos*, meaning reason. Although we humans do not always think alike or have the same degree of reason, Heraclitus believed that there must be a kind of 'universal reason' guiding everything that happens in nature.

This 'universal reason' or 'universal law' is something common to us all, and something that everybody is guided by. And yet most people live by their individual reason, thought Heraclitus. In general, he despised his fellow beings. 'The opinions of most people,' he said, 'are like the play-things of infants.'

So in the midst of all nature's constant flux and opposites, Heraclitus saw an Entity or one-ness. This 'something,' which was the source of everything, he called God or *logos*.

Four Basic Elements
In one way, Parmenides and Heraclitus were the direct opposite of each other. Parmenides' *reason* made it clear that nothing could change. Heraclitus' *sense perceptions* made it equally clear that nature was in a constant state of change. Which of them was right? Should we let reason dictate or should we rely on our senses?

Parmenides and Heraclitus both say two things:
Parmenides says:
  a) that nothing can change, and
  b) that our sensory perceptions must therefore be unreliable.

Heraclitus, on the other hand, says:
   a) that everything changes ('all things flow'), and
   b) that our sensory perceptions are reliable.

Philosophers could hardly disagree more than that! But who was right? It fell to *Empedocles* (c. 490–430 B.C.) from Sicily to lead the way out of the tangle they had gotten themselves into.

He thought they were both right in one of their assertions but wrong in the other.

Empedocles found that the cause of their basic disagreement was that both philosophers had assumed the presence of only *one* element. If this were true, the gap between what reason dictates and what 'we can see with our own eyes' would be unbridgeable.

Water obviously cannot turn into a fish or a butterfly. In fact, water cannot change. Pure water will continue to be pure water. So Parmenides was right in holding that 'nothing changes.'

But at the same time Empedocles agreed with Heraclitus that we must trust the evidence of our senses. We must believe what we see, and what we see is precisely that nature changes.

Empedocles concluded that it was the idea of a single basic substance that had to be rejected. Neither water nor air *alone* can change into a rosebush or a butterfly. The source of nature cannot possibly be one single 'element.'

Empedocles believed that all in all, nature consisted of four elements, or 'roots' as he termed them. These four

roots were *earth, air, fire,* and *water.*

All natural processes were due to the coming together and separating of these four elements. For all things were a mixture of earth, air, fire, and water, but in varying proportions. When a flower or an animal dies, he said, the four elements separate again. We can register these changes with the naked eye. But earth and air, fire and water remain everlasting, 'untouched' by all the compounds of which they are part. So it is not correct to say that 'everything' changes. Basically, nothing changes. What happens is that the four elements are combined and separated – only to be combined again.

We can make a comparison to painting. If a painter only has one color – red, for instance – he cannot paint green trees. But if he has yellow, red, blue, and black, he can paint in hundreds of different colors because he can mix them in varying proportions.

An example from the kitchen illustrates the same thing. If I only have flour, I have to be a wizard to bake a cake. But if I have eggs, flour, milk, and sugar, then I can make any number of different cakes.

It was not purely by chance that Empedocles chose earth, air, fire, and water as nature's 'roots.' Other philosophers before him had tried to show that the primordial substance had to be either water, air, or fire. Thales and Anaximenes had pointed out that both water and air were essential elements in the physical world. The Greeks believed that fire was also essential. They observed, for example, the importance of the sun to all living things, and they also knew that both animals and humans have body heat.

Empedocles might have watched a piece of wood burning.

Something disintegrates. We hear it crackle and splutter. That is 'water.' Something goes up in smoke. That is 'air.' The 'fire' we can see. Something also remains when the fire is extinguished. That is the ashes – or 'earth.'

After Empedocles' clarification of nature's transformations as the combination and dissolution of the four 'roots,' something still remained to be explained. What makes these elements combine so that new life can occur? And what makes the 'mixture' of, say, a flower dissolve again?

Empedocles believed that there were two different *forces* at work in nature. He called them *love* and *strife*. Love binds things together, and strife separates them.

He distinguishes between 'substance' and 'force.' This is worth noting. Even today, scientists distinguish between *elements* and *natural forces*. Modern science holds that all natural processes can be explained as the interaction between different elements and various natural forces.

Empedocles also raised the question of what happens when we perceive something. How can I 'see' a flower, for example? What is it that happens?

Empedocles believed that the eyes consist of earth, air, fire, and water, just like everything else in nature. So the 'earth' in my eye perceives what is of the earth in my surroundings, the 'air' perceives what is of the air, the 'fire' perceives what is of fire, and the 'water' what is of water. Had my eyes lacked any of the four substances, I would not have seen all of nature.

Something of Everything in Everything

Anaxagoras (500–428 B.C.) was another philosopher who could not agree that one particular basic substance – water, for instance – might be transformed into everything we see in the natural world. Nor could he accept that earth, air, fire, and water can be transformed into blood and bone.

Anaxagoras held that nature is built up of an infinite number of minute particles invisible to the eye. Moreover, everything can be divided into even smaller parts, but even in the minutest parts there are fragments of all other things. If skin and bone are not a transformation of something else, there must also be skin and bone, he thought, in the milk we drink and the food we eat.

A couple of present-day examples can perhaps illustrate Anaxagoras' line of thinking. Modern laser technology can produce so-called holograms. If one of these holograms depicts a car, for example, and the hologram is fragmented, we will see a picture of the whole car even though we only have the part of the hologram that showed the bumper. This is because the whole subject is present in every tiny part.

In a sense, our bodies are built up in the same way. If I loosen a skin cell from my finger, the nucleus will contain not only the characteristics of my skin: the same cell will also reveal what kind of eyes I have, the color of my hair, the number and type of my fingers, and so on. Every cell of the human body carries a blueprint of the way all the other cells are constructed. So there is 'something of everything' in every single cell. The whole exists in each tiny part.

Anaxagoras called these minuscule particles which have something of everything in them *seeds*.

Remember that Empedocles thought that it was 'love' that joined the elements together in whole bodies. Anaxagoras also imagined 'order' as a kind of force, creating animals and humans, flowers and trees. He called this force mind or intelligence (nous).

Anaxagoras is also interesting because he was the first philosopher we hear of in Athens. He was from Asia Minor but he moved to Athens at the age of forty. He was later accused of atheism and was ultimately forced to leave the city. Among other things, he said that the sun was not a god but a red-hot stone, bigger than the entire Peloponnesian peninsula.

Anaxagoras was generally very interested in astronomy. He believed that all heavenly bodies were made of the same substance as Earth. He reached this conclusion after studying a meteorite. This gave him the idea that there could be human life on other planets. He also pointed out that the Moon has no light of its own – its light comes from Earth, he said. He thought up an explanation for solar eclipses as well.

DEMOCRITUS

The Atom Theory

Democritus agreed with his predecessors that transformations in nature could not be due to the fact that anything actually 'changed.' He therefore assumed that everything was built up of tiny invisible blocks, each of which was eternal and immutable. Democritus called these smallest units *atoms*.

The word 'a-tom' means 'un-cuttable.' For Democritus it was all-important to establish that the constituent parts that everything else was composed of could not be divided indefinitely into smaller parts. If this were possible, they could not be used as blocks. If atoms could eternally be broken down into ever smaller parts, nature would begin to dissolve like constantly diluted soup.

Moreover, nature's blocks had to be eternal – because nothing can come from nothing. In this, he agreed with Parmenides and the Eleatics. Also, he believed that all atoms were firm and solid. But they could not all be the same. If all atoms were identical, there would still be no satisfactory explanation of how they could combine to form everything from poppies and olive trees to goatskin and human hair.

Democritus believed that nature consisted of an unlimited number and variety of atoms. Some were round and smooth, others were irregular and jagged. And precisely because they were so different they could join together into all kinds of different bodies. But however infinite they might be in number and shape, they were all eternal, immutable, and indivisible.

When a body – a tree or an animal, for instance – died and disintegrated, the atoms dispersed and could be used again in new bodies. Atoms moved around in space, but because they had 'hooks' and 'barbs,' they could join together to form all the things we see around us.

Today we can establish that Democritus' atom theory was more or less correct. Nature really is built up of different 'atoms' that join and separate again. A hydrogen atom in a cell at the end of my nose was once part of an elephant's trunk. A carbon atom in my cardiac muscle was once in the tail of a dinosaur.

In our own time, however, scientists have discovered that atoms can be broken into smaller 'elemental particles.' We call these elemental particles protons, neutrons, and electrons. These will possibly some day be broken into even lesser particles. But physicists agree that somewhere along the line there has to be a limit. There has to be a 'minimal part' of which nature consists.

Democritus did not have access to modern electronic apparatus. His only proper equipment was his mind. But reason left him no real choice. Once it is accepted that nothing can change, that nothing can come out of nothing, and that nothing is ever lost, then nature *must* consist of infinitesimal blocks that can join and separate again.

Democritus did not believe in any 'force' or 'soul' that could intervene in natural processes. The only things that existed, he believed, were atoms and the void. Since he believed in nothing but material things, we call him a *materialist*.

According to Democritus, there is no conscious 'design'

in the movement of atoms. In nature, everything happens quite mechanically. This does not mean that everything happens randomly, for everything obeys the inevitable laws of necessity. Everything that happens has a natural cause, a cause that is inherent in the thing itself. Democritus once said that he would rather discover a new cause of nature than be the King of Persia.

The atom theory also explains our *sense perception*, thought Democritus. When we sense something, it is due to the movement of atoms in space. When I see the moon, it is because 'moon atoms' penetrate my eye.

But what about the 'soul,' then? Surely that could not consist of atoms, of material things? Indeed it could. Democritus believed that the soul was made up of special round, smooth 'soul atoms.' When a human being died, the soul atoms flew in all directions, and could then become part of a new soul formation.

This meant that human beings had no immortal soul, another belief that many people share today. They believe, like Democritus, that 'soul' is connected with brain, and that we cannot have any form of consciousness once the brain disintegrates.

Democritus's atom theory marked the end of Greek natural philosophy for the time being. He agreed with Heraclitus that everything in nature 'flowed,' since forms come and go. But behind everything that flowed there were some eternal and immutable things that did not flow. Democritus called them atoms.

FATE

We have seen how philosophers tried to find natural explanations for the transformations in Nature. Previously these things had been explained through myths.

Old superstitions had to be cleared away in other areas as well. We see them at work in matters of sickness and health as well as in political events. In both these areas the Greeks were great believers in *fatalism*.

Fatalism is the belief that whatever happens is predestined. We find this belief all over the world, not only throughout history but in our own day as well. Here in the Nordic countries we find a strong belief in 'lagnadan,' or fate, in the old Icelandic sagas of the *Edda*.

We also find the belief, both in Ancient Greece and in other parts of the world, that people could learn their fate from some form of *oracle*. In other words, that the fate of a person or a country could be foreseen in various ways.

There are still a lot of people who believe that they can tell your fortune in the cards, read your palm, or predict your future in the stars.

A special Norwegian version of this is telling your fortune in coffee cups. When a coffee cup is empty there are usually some traces of coffee grounds left. These might form a certain image or pattern – at least, if we give our imagination free rein. If the grounds resemble a car, it might mean that the person who drank from the cup is going for a long drive.

Thus the 'fortune-teller' is trying to foresee something that is really quite unforeseeable. This is characteristic of all forms of foreseeing. And precisely because what they 'see' is so vague, it is hard to repudiate fortune-tellers' claims.

When we gaze up at the stars, we see a veritable chaos of twinkling dots. Nevertheless, throughout the ages there have always been people who believed that the stars could tell us something about our life on Earth. Even today there are political leaders who seek the advice of astrologers before they make any important decisions.

The Oracle at Delphi

The ancient Greeks believed that they could consult the famous oracle at Delphi about their fate. Apollo, the god of the oracle, spoke through his priestess Pythia, who sat on a stool over a fissure in the earth, from which arose hypnotic vapors that put Pythia in a trance. This enabled her to be Apollo's mouthpiece.

When people came to Delphi they had to present their question to the priests of the oracle, who passed it on to Pythia. Her answer would be so obscure or ambiguous that the priests would have to interpret it. In that way, the people got the benefit of Apollo's wisdom, believing that he knew everything, even about the future.

There were many heads of state who dared not go to war or take other decisive steps until they had consulted the oracle at Delphi. The priests of Apollo thus functioned more or less as diplomats, or advisers. They were experts with an intimate knowledge of the people and the country.

Over the entrance to the temple at Delphi was a famous inscription: KNOW THYSELF! It reminded visitors that man must never believe himself to be more than mortal – and that no man can escape his destiny.

The Greeks had many stories of people whose destiny catches up with them. As time went by, a number of plays – tragedies – were written about these 'tragic' people. The most famous one is the tragedy of King Oedipus.

History and Medicine

But Fate did not just govern the lives of individuals. The Greeks believed that even world history was governed by Fate, and that the fortunes of war could be swayed by the intervention of the gods. Today there are still many people who believe that God or some other mysterious power is steering the course of history.

But at the same time as Greek philosophers were trying to find natural explanations for the processes of nature, the first historians were beginning to search for natural explanations for the course of history. When a country lost a war, the vengeance of the gods was no longer an acceptable explanation to them. The best known Greek historians were *Herodotus* (484–424 B.C.) and *Thucydides* (460–400 B.C.).

The Greeks also believed that sickness could be ascribed to divine intervention. On the other hand, the gods could make people well again if they made the appropriate sacrifices.

This idea was in no way unique to the Greeks. Before the development of modern medicine, the most widely accepted view was that sickness was due to supernatural causes. The word 'influenza' actually means a malign influence from the stars.

Even today, there are a lot of people who believe that some diseases – AIDS, for example – are God's punishment. Many also believe that sick people can be cured with the help of the supernatural.

Concurrently with the new directions in Greek philosophy, a Greek medical science arose which tried to find natural explanations for sickness and health. The founder of Greek medicine is said to have been *Hippocrates,* who was born on the island of Cos around 460 B.C.

The most essential safeguards against sickness, according to the Hippocratic medical tradition, were moderation and a healthy lifestyle. Health is the natural condition. When sickness occurs, it is a sign that Nature has gone off course because of physical or mental imbalance. The road to health for everyone is through moderation, harmony, and a 'sound mind in a sound body.'

There is a lot of talk today about 'medical ethics,' which is another way of saying that a doctor must practice medicine according to certain ethical rules. For instance, a doctor may not give healthy people a prescription for narcotics. A doctor must also maintain professional secrecy, which means that he is not allowed to reveal anything a patient has told him about his illness. These ideas go back to Hippocrates. He required his pupils to take the following oath:

> I will follow that system or regimen which, according to my ability and judgment, I consider to be for the benefit of my patients, and abstain from whatever is deleterious and mischievous. I will give no deadly medicine to anyone 19

if asked nor suggest any such counsel, and in like manner I will not give to a woman the means to produce an abortion. Whenever I go into a house, I will go for the benefit of the sick and will abstain from every voluntary act of mischief and corruption, and further, from the seduction of females or males, whether freemen or slaves. Whatever, in connection with my professional practice, I see or hear which ought not to be spoken abroad, I will keep secret. So long as I continue to carry out this oath unviolated, may it be granted to me to enjoy life and the practice of the art, respected by all men in all times, but should I violate this oath, may the reverse be my lot.

The Philosophy of Athens

Now we are going to meet the three great classical philosophers, Socrates, Plato, and Aristotle. Each in his own way, these philosophers influenced the whole of European civilization.

The natural philosophers are also called the pre-Socratics, because they lived before Socrates. Although Democritus died some years after Socrates, all his ideas belong to pre-Socratic natural philosophy. Socrates represents a new era, geographically as well as temporally. He was the first of the great philosophers to be born in Athens, and both he and his two successors lived and worked there. You may recall that Anaxagoras also lived in Athens for a while but was hounded out because he said the sun was a red-hot stone. (Socrates fared no better!)

From the time of Socrates, Athens was the center of Greek culture. It is also important to note the change of character in the philosophical project itself as it progresses from natural philosophy to Socrates. But before we meet Socrates, let us hear a little about the so-called Sophists, who dominated the Athenian scene at the time of Socrates.

Man at the Center

After about 450 B.C., Athens was the cultural center of the Greek world. From this time on, philosophy took a new direction.

The natural philosophers had been mainly concerned with the nature of the physical world. This gives them a central position in the history of science. In Athens, interest was now focused on the individual and the individual's place in society. Gradually a democracy evolved, with popular assemblies and courts of law.

In order for democracy to work, people had to be educated enough to take part in the democratic process. We have seen in our own time how a young democracy needs popular enlightenment. For the Athenians, it was first and foremost essential to master the art of rhetoric, which means saying things in a convincing manner.

A group of itinerant teachers and philosophers from the Greek colonies flocked to Athens. They called themselves *Sophists*. The word 'sophist' means a wise and informed person. In Athens, the Sophists made a living out of teaching the citizens for money.

The Sophists had one characteristic in common with the natural philosophers: they were critical of the traditional mythology. But at the same time the Sophists rejected what they regarded as fruitless philosophical speculation. Their opinion was that although answers to philosophical questions may exist, man cannot know the truth about the riddles of nature and of the universe. In philosophy a view like this is called *skepticism*.

22   But even if we cannot know the answers to all of nature's

riddles, we know that people have to learn to live together. The Sophists chose to concern themselves with man and his place in society.

'Man is the measure of all things,' said the Sophist *Protagoras* (c. 485–410 B.C.). By that he meant that the question of whether a thing is right or wrong, good or bad, must always be considered in relation to a person's needs. On being asked whether he believed in the Greek gods, he answered, 'The question is complex and life is short.' A person who is unable to say categorically whether or not the gods or God exists is called an *agnostic*.

The Sophists were as a rule men who had traveled widely and seen different forms of government. Both conventions and local laws in the city-states could vary widely. This led the Sophists to raise the question of what was *natural* and what was *socially induced*. By doing this, they paved the way for social criticism in the city-state of Athens.

They could for example point out that the use of an expression like 'natural modesty' is not always defensible, for if it is 'natural' to be modest, it must be something you are born with, something innate. But is it really innate, or is it socially induced? To someone who has traveled the world, the answer should be simple: It is not 'natural' – or innate – to be afraid to show yourself naked. Modesty – or the lack of it – is first and foremost a matter of social convention.

As you can imagine, the wandering Sophists created bitter wrangling in Athens by pointing out that there were no *absolute norms* for what was right or wrong.

Socrates, on the other hand, tried to show that some such

norms *are* in fact absolute and universally valid.

Who Was Socrates?

Socrates (470–399 B.C.) is possibly the most enigmatic figure in the entire history of philosophy. He never wrote a single line. Yet he is one of the philosophers who has had the greatest influence on European thought, not least because of the dramatic manner of his death.

We know he was born in Athens, and that he spent most of his life in the city squares and marketplaces talking with the people he met there. 'The trees in the countryside can teach me nothing,' he said. He could also stand lost in thought for hours on end.

Even during his lifetime he was considered somewhat enigmatic, and fairly soon after his death he was held to be the founder of any number of different philosophical schools of thought. The very fact that he was so enigmatic and ambiguous made it possible for widely differing schools of thought to claim him as their own.

We know for a certainty that he was extremely ugly. He was potbellied, and had bulging eyes and a snub nose. But inside he was said to be 'perfectly delightful.' It was also said of him that 'You can seek him in the present, you can seek him in the past, but you will never find his equal.' Nevertheless he was sentenced to death for his philosophical activities.

The life of Socrates is mainly known to us through the writings of Plato, who was one of his pupils and who became one of the greatest philosophers of all time. Plato wrote a number of *Dialogues*, or dramatized discussions on philosophy, in which he uses Socrates as his principal character and mouthpiece.

Since Plato is putting his own philosophy in Socrates' mouth, we cannot be sure that the words he speaks in the dialogues were ever actually uttered by him. So it is no easy matter to distinguish between the teachings of Socrates and the philosophy of Plato. Exactly the same problem applies to many other historical persons who left no written accounts. The classic example, of course, is Jesus. We cannot be certain that the 'historical' Jesus actually spoke the words that Matthew or Luke ascribed to him. Similarly, what the 'historical' Socrates actually said will always be shrouded in mystery.

But who Socrates 'really' was is relatively unimportant. It is Plato's portrait of Socrates that has inspired thinkers in the Western world for nearly 2,500 years.

The Art of Discourse

The essential nature of Socrates' art lay in the fact that he did not appear to want to instruct people. On the contrary he gave the impression of one desiring to learn from those he spoke with. So instead of lecturing like a traditional schoolmaster, he *discussed*.

Obviously he would not have become a famous philosopher had he confined himself purely to listening to others. Nor would he have been sentenced to death. But he just asked questions, especially to begin a conversation, as if he knew nothing. In the course of the discussion he would generally get his opponents to recognize the weakness of their arguments, and, forced into a corner, they would finally be obliged to realize what was right and what was wrong.

Socrates, whose mother was a midwife, used to say that his art was like the art of the midwife. She does not herself give birth to the child, but she is there to help during its delivery. Similarly, Socrates saw his task as helping people to 'give birth' to the correct insight, since real understanding must come from within. It cannot be imparted by someone else. And only the understanding that comes from within can lead to true insight.

Let me put it more precisely: The ability to give birth is a natural characteristic. In the same way, everybody can grasp philosophical truths if they just use their innate reason. Using your innate reason means reaching down inside yourself and using what is there.

By playing ignorant, Socrates forced the people he met to use their common sense. Socrates could feign ignorance – or pretend to be dumber than he was. We call this Socratic irony. This enabled him to continually expose the weaknesses in people's thinking. He was not averse to doing this in the middle of the city square. If you met Socrates, you thus might end up being made a fool of publicly.

So it is not surprising that, as time went by, people found him increasingly exasperating, especially people who had status in the community. 'Athens is like a sluggish horse,' he is reputed to have said, 'and I am the gadfly trying to sting it into life.'

A Divine Voice

It was not in order to torment his fellow beings that Socrates kept on stinging them. Something within him left him no choice. He always said that he had a 'divine voice' inside him. Socrates protested, for example, against having any part in condemning people to death. He moreover refused to inform on his political enemies. This was eventually to cost him his life.

In the year 399 B.C. he was accused of 'introducing new gods and corrupting the youth,' as well as not believing in the accepted gods. With a slender majority, a jury of five hundred found him guilty.

He could very likely have appealed for leniency. At least he could have saved his life by agreeing to leave Athens. But had he done this he would not have been Socrates. He valued his conscience – and the truth – higher than life. He assured the jury that he had only acted in the best interests of the state. He was nevertheless condemned to drink hemlock. Shortly thereafter, he drank the poison in the presence of his friends, and died.

Why did Socrates have to die? People have been asking this question for 2,400 years. However, he was not the only person in history to have seen things through to the bitter end and suffered death for the sake of their convictions.

I have mentioned Jesus already, and in fact there are several striking parallels between them.

Both Jesus and Socrates were enigmatic personalities, also to their contemporaries. Neither of them wrote down their teachings, so we are forced to rely on the picture we have of them from their disciples. But we do know that they were both masters of the art of discourse. They both spoke with a characteristic self-assuredness that could fascinate as well as exasperate. And not least, they both believed that they spoke on behalf of something greater than themselves. They challenged the power of the community by criticizing all forms of injustice and corruption. And finally – their activities cost them their lives.

The trials of Jesus and Socrates also exhibit clear parallels.

They could certainly both have saved themselves by appealing for mercy, but they both felt they had a mission that would have been betrayed unless they kept faith to the bitter end. And by meeting their deaths so bravely they commanded an enormous following, also after they had died.

I do not mean to suggest that Jesus and Socrates were alike. I am merely drawing attention to the fact that they both had a message that was inseparably linked to their personal courage.

A Joker in Athens

Socrates lived at the same time as the Sophists. Like them, he was more concerned with man and his place in society than with the forces of nature. As a Roman philosopher, Cicero, said of him a few hundred years later, Socrates 'called philosophy down from the sky and established her in the towns and introduced her into homes and forced her to investigate life, ethics, good and evil.'

But Socrates differed from the Sophists in one significant

way. He did not consider himself to be a 'sophist' – that is, a learned or wise person. Unlike the Sophists, he did not teach for money. No, Socrates called himself a philosopher in the true sense of the word. A 'philo-sopher' really means 'one who loves wisdom.'

The Sophists took money for their more or less hair-splitting expoundings, and sophists of this kind have come and gone from time immemorial. I am referring to all the schoolmasters and self-opinionated know-it-alls who are satisfied with what little they know, or who boast of knowing a whole lot about subjects they haven't the faintest notion of. A real *philosopher* is a completely different kettle of fish – the direct opposite, in fact. A philosopher knows that in reality he knows very little. That is why he constantly strives to achieve true insight. Socrates was one of these rare people. He *knew* that he knew nothing about life and about the world. And now comes the important part: it troubled him that he knew so little.

A philosopher is therefore someone who recognizes that there is a lot he does not understand, and is troubled by it. In that sense, he is still wiser than all those who brag about their knowledge of things they know nothing about. 'Wisest is she who knows she does not know,' I said previously. Socrates himself said, 'One thing only I know, and that is that I know nothing.'

Remember this statement, because it is an admission that is rare, even among philosophers. Moreover, it can be so dangerous to say it in public that it can cost you your life. The most subversive people are those who ask questions. Giving answers is not nearly as threatening. Any one question can be more explosive than a thousand answers.

You remember the story of the emperor's new clothes? The emperor was actually stark naked but none of his subjects dared say so. Suddenly a child burst out, 'But he's got nothing on!' That was a *courageous* child. Like Socrates, who dared tell people how little we humans know. The similarity between children and philosophers is something we have already talked about.

To be precise: Mankind is faced with a number of difficult questions that we have no satisfactory answers to. So now two possibilities present themselves: We can either fool ourselves and the rest of the world by pretending that we know all there is to know, or we can shut our eyes to the central issues once and for all and abandon all progress. In this sense, humanity is divided. People are, generally speaking, either dead certain or totally indifferent.

It is like dividing a deck of cards into two piles. You lay the black cards in one pile and the red in the other. But from time to time a joker turns up that is neither heart nor club, neither diamond nor spade. Socrates was this joker in Athens. He was neither certain nor indifferent. All he knew was that he knew nothing – and it troubled him. So he became a philosopher – someone who does not give up but tirelessly pursues his quest for truth.

An Athenian is said to have asked the oracle at Delphi who the wisest man in Athens was. The oracle answered that Socrates of all mortals was the wisest. When Socrates heard this he was astounded, to put it mildly. He went straight to the person in the city whom he, and everyone else, thought was excessively wise. But when it turned out that this person was unable to give Socrates satisfactory answers to his questions, Socrates realized that the oracle had been right.

Socrates felt that it was necessary to establish a solid foundation for our knowledge. He believed that this foundation lay in man's reason. With his unshakable faith in human reason he was decidedly a *rationalist*.

The Right Insight Leads to the Right Action

As I have mentioned earlier, Socrates claimed that he was guided by a divine inner voice, and that this 'conscience' told him what was right. 'He who knows what good is will do good,' he said.

By this he meant that the right insight leads to the right action. And only he who does right can be a 'virtuous man.' When we do wrong it is because we don't know any better. That is why it is so important to go on learning. Socrates was concerned with finding clear and universally valid definitions of right and wrong. Unlike the Sophists, he believed that the ability to distinguish between right and wrong lies in people's reason and not in society.

You may perhaps think this last part is a bit too obscure. Let me put it like this: Socrates thought that no one could possibly be happy if they acted against their better judgment. And he who knows how to achieve happiness will do so. Therefore, he who knows what is right will do right. Because why would anybody choose to be unhappy?

Can you live a happy life if you continually do things you know deep down are wrong? There are lots of people who lie and cheat and speak ill of others. Are they aware that these things are not right – or fair, if you prefer? Do you think these people are happy?

Socrates didn't.

Plato's Academy

Plato (428–347 B.C.) was twenty-nine years old when Socrates drank the hemlock. He had been a pupil of Socrates for some time and had followed his trial very closely. The fact that Athens could condemn its noblest citizen to death did more than make a profound impression on him. It was to shape the course of his entire philosophic endeavor.

To Plato, the death of Socrates was a striking example of the conflict that can exist between society as it really is and the *true* or *ideal* society. Plato's first deed as a philosopher was to publish Socrates' *Apology*, an account of his plea to the large jury.

As you will no doubt recall, Socrates never wrote anything down, although many of the pre-Socratics did. The problem is that hardly any of their written material remains. But in the case of Plato, we believe that all his principal works have been preserved. (In addition to Socrates' *Apology*, Plato wrote a collection of *Epistles* and about twenty-five philosophical *Dialogues*.) That we have these works today is due not least to the fact that Plato set up his own school of philosophy in a grove not far from Athens, named after the legendary Greek hero Academus. The school was therefore known as the Academy. (Since then, many thousands of 'academies' have been established all over the world. We still speak of 'academics' and 'academic subjects.')

The subjects taught at Plato's Academy were philosophy, mathematics, and gymnastics – although perhaps 'taught' is hardly the right word. Lively discourse was considered most important at Plato's Academy. So it was not purely by chance that Plato's writings took the form of dialogues.

The Eternally True, Eternally Beautiful, and Eternally Good

Briefly, we can establish that Plato was concerned with the relationship between what is eternal and immutable, on the one hand, and what 'flows,' on the other. (Just like the pre-Socratics, in fact.) We've seen how the Sophists and Socrates turned their attention from questions of natural philosophy to problems related to man and society. And yet in one sense, even Socrates and the Sophists were preoccupied with the relationship between the eternal and immutable, and the 'flowing.' They were interested in the problem as it related to human *morals* and society's ideals or virtues. Very briefly, the Sophists thought that perceptions of what was right or wrong varied from one city-state to another, and from one generation to the next. So right and wrong was something that 'flowed.' This was totally unacceptable to Socrates. He believed in the existence of eternal and absolute rules for what was right or wrong. By using our common sense we can all arrive at these immutable *norms*, since human reason is in fact eternal and immutable.

Then along comes Plato. He is concerned with *both* what is eternal and immutable in nature *and* what is eternal and immutable as regards morals and society. To Plato, these 33 two problems were one and the same. He tried to grasp a 'reality' that was eternal and immutable.

And to be quite frank, that is precisely what we need philosophers for. We do not need them to choose a beauty queen or the day's bargain in tomatoes. (This is why they are often unpopular!) Philosophers will try to ignore highly topical affairs and instead try to draw people's attention to what is eternally 'true,' eternally 'beautiful,' and eternally 'good.'

We can thus begin to glimpse at least the outline of Plato's philosophical project. But let's take one thing at a time. We are attempting to understand an extraordinary mind, a mind that was to have a profound influence on all subsequent European philosophy.

The World of Ideas
Both Empedocles and Democritus had drawn attention to the fact that although in the natural world everything 'flows,' there must nevertheless be 'something' that never changes (the 'four roots,' or the 'atoms'). Plato agreed with the proposition as such – but in quite a different way.

Plato believed that *everything* tangible in nature 'flows.' So there are no 'substances' that do not dissolve. Absolutely everything that belongs to the 'material world' is made of a material that time can erode, but everything is made after a timeless 'mold' or 'form' that is eternal and immutable.

Why are horses the same? You probably don't think they are at all. But there is something that all horses have in common, something that enables us to identify them as horses. A particular horse 'flows,' naturally. It might be old and lame, and in time it will die. But the 'form' of the horse is eternal and immutable.

That which is eternal and immutable, to Plato, is therefore not a physical 'basic substance,' as it was for Empedocles and Democritus. Plato's conception was of eternal and immutable patterns, spiritual and abstract in their nature, that all things are fashioned after.

Let me put it like this: The pre-Socratics had given a reasonably good explanation of natural change without having to presuppose that anything actually 'changed.' In the midst of nature's cycle there were some eternal and immutable smallest elements that did not dissolve, they thought. But they had no reasonable explanation for *how* these 'smallest elements' that were once building blocks in a horse could suddenly whirl together four or five hundred years later and fashion themselves into a completely new horse. Or an elephant or a crocodile, for that matter. Plato's point was that Democritus' atoms never fashioned themselves into an 'eledile' or a 'crocophant.' This was what set his philosophical reflections going.

If you already understand what I am getting at, you may skip this next paragraph. But just in case, I will clarify: You have a box of Lego and you build a Lego horse. You then take it apart and put the blocks back in the box. You cannot expect to make a new horse just by shaking the box. How could Lego blocks of their own accord find each other and become a new horse again? No, *you* have to rebuild the horse. And the reason you can do it is that you have a picture in your mind of what the horse looked like. The

Lego horse is made from a model which remains unchanged from horse to horse.

Let us assume that you have dropped in from outer space and have never seen a baker before. You stumble into a tempting bakery – and there you catch sight of fifty identical gingerbread men on a shelf. I imagine you would wonder how they could be exactly alike. It might well be that one of them has an arm missing, another has lost a bit of its head, and a third has a funny bump on its stomach. But after careful thought, you would nevertheless conclude that all gingerbread men have something *in common*. Although none of them is perfect, you would suspect that they had a common origin. You would realize that all the cookies were formed in the same mold. And what is more, you are now seized by the irresistible desire to see this mold. Because clearly, the mold itself must be utter perfection – and in a sense, more beautiful – in comparison with these crude copies.

Like most philosophers, he 'dropped in from outer space.' He was astonished at the way all natural phenomena could be so alike, and he concluded that it had to be because there are a limited number of *forms* 'behind' everything we see around us. Plato called these forms *ideas*. Behind every horse, pig, or human being, there is the 'idea horse,' 'idea pig,' and 'idea human being.' (In the same way, the bakery we spoke of can have gingerbread men, gingerbread horses, and gingerbread pigs. Because every self-respecting bakery has more than one mold. But one mold is enough for each *type* of gingerbread cookie.)

Plato came to the conclusion that there must be a reality

behind the 'material world.' He called this reality *the world of ideas*; it contained the eternal and immutable 'patterns' behind the various phenomena we come across in nature. This remarkable view is known as Plato's *theory of ideas*.

True Knowledge

I'm sure you've been following me. But you may be wondering whether Plato was being serious. Did he really believe that forms like these actually existed in a completely different reality?

He probably didn't believe it literally in the same way for all his life, but in some of his dialogues that is certainly how he means to be understood. Let us try to follow his train of thought.

A philosopher, as we have seen, tries to grasp something that is eternal and immutable. It would serve no purpose, for instance, to write a philosophic treatise on the existence of a particular soap bubble. Partly because one would hardly have time to study it in depth before it burst, and partly because it would probably be rather difficult to find a market for a philosophic treatise on something nobody has ever seen, and which only existed for five seconds.

Plato believed that everything we see around us in nature, everything tangible, can be likened to a soap bubble, since nothing that exists in the world of the senses is lasting. We know, of course, that sooner or later every human being and every animal will die and decompose. Even a block of marble changes and gradually disintegrates. Plato's point is that we can never have true knowledge of anything that is in a constant state of change. We can only have *opinions* about things that belong to the world of the senses, tangible things. We can only have true *knowledge* of things that can be understood with our reason.

All right, I'll explain it more clearly: a gingerbread man can be so lopsided after all that baking that it can be quite hard to see what it is meant to be. But having seen dozens of gingerbread men that were more or less successful, I can be pretty sure what the cookie mold was like. I can guess, even though I have never seen it. It might not even be an advantage to see the actual mold with my own eyes because we cannot always trust the evidence of our senses. The faculty of vision can vary from person to person. On the other hand, we can rely on what our reason tells us because that is the same for everyone.

If you are sitting in a classroom with thirty other pupils, and the teacher asks the class which color of the rainbow is the prettiest, he will probably get a lot of different answers. But if he asks what 8 times 3 is, the whole class will – we hope – give the same answer. Because now reason is speaking and reason is, in a way, the direct opposite of 'thinking so' or 'feeling.' We could say that reason is eternal and universal precisely because it only expresses eternal and universal states.

Plato found mathematics very absorbing because mathematical states never change. They are therefore states we can have true knowledge of. But here we need an example.

Imagine you find a round pinecone out in the woods. Perhaps you say you 'think' it looks completely round, whereas someone else insists it is a bit flattened on one side. (Then you start arguing about it!) But you cannot have true knowledge of anything you can perceive with your eyes. On the other hand you can say with absolute certainty that the sum of the angles in a circle is 360 degrees. In this case you would be talking about an *ideal* circle which might not exist in the physical world but which you can clearly visualize. (You are dealing with the hidden gingerbread-man mold and not with the particular cookie on the kitchen table.)

In short, we can only have inexact conceptions of things we perceive with our senses. But we can have true knowledge of things we *understand* with our reason. The sum of the angles in a triangle will remain 180 degrees to the end of time. And similarly the 'idea' horse will walk on four legs even if all the horses in the sensory world break a leg.

An Immortal Soul
As I explained, Plato believed that reality is divided into two regions.

One region is the *world of the senses*, about which we can only have approximate or incomplete knowledge by using our five (approximate or incomplete) senses. In this sensory world, 'everything flows' and nothing is permanent. Nothing in the sensory world *is*, there are only things that come to be and pass away.

The other region is the *world of ideas*, about which we can have true knowledge by using our reason. This world of ideas cannot be perceived by the senses, but the ideas (or forms) are eternal and immutable.

According to Plato, man is a dual creature. We have a body

that 'flows,' is inseparably bound to the world of the senses, and is subject to the same fate as everything else in this world – a soap bubble, for example. All our senses are based in the body and are consequently unreliable. But we also have an immortal *soul* – and this soul is the realm of reason. And not being physical, the soul can survey the world of ideas.

But that's not all. IT'S NOT ALL!

Plato also believed that the soul existed *before* it inhabited the body. (It was lying on a shelf in the closet with all the cookie molds.) But as soon as the soul wakes up in a human body, it has forgotten all the perfect ideas. Then something starts to happen. In fact, a wondrous process begins. As the human being discovers the various forms in the natural world, a vague recollection stirs his soul. He sees a horse – but an imperfect horse. (A gingerbread horse!) The sight of it is sufficient to awaken in the soul a faint recollection of the perfect 'horse,' which the soul once saw in the world of ideas, and this stirs the soul with a yearning to return to its true realm. Plato calls this yearning *eros* – which means love. The soul, then, experiences a 'longing to return to its true origin.' From now on, the body and the whole sensory world is experienced as imperfect and insignificant. The soul yearns to fly home on the wings of love to the world of ideas. It longs to be freed from the chains of the body.

Let me quickly emphasize that Plato is describing an ideal course of life, since by no means all humans set the soul free to begin its journey back to the world of ideas. Most people cling to the sensory world's 'reflections' of ideas. They see a horse – and another horse. But they never see that of which every horse is only a feeble imitation. (They rush into the kitchen and stuff themselves with gingerbread cookies without so much as a thought as to where they came from.) What Plato describes is the *philosophers'* way. His philosophy can be read as a description of philosophic practice.

When you see a shadow, you will assume that there must be something casting the shadow. You see the shadow of an animal. You think it may be a horse, but you are not quite sure. So you turn around and see the horse itself – which of course is infinitely more beautiful and sharper in outline than the blurred 'horse-shadow.' *Plato believed similarly that all natural phenomena are merely shadows of the eternal forms or ideas.* But most people are content with a life among shadows. They give no thought to what is casting the shadows. They think shadows are all there are, never realizing even that they are, in fact, shadows. And thus they pay no heed to the immortality of their own soul.

Out of the Darkness of the Cave
Plato relates a myth which illustrates this. We call it the *Myth of the Cave*. I'll retell it in my own words.

Imagine some people living in an underground cave. They sit with their backs to the mouth of the cave with their hands and feet bound in such a way that they can only look at the back wall of the cave. Behind them is a high wall, and behind that wall pass human-like creatures, holding up various figures above the top of the wall. Because there is a fire behind these figures, they cast flickering shadows on the back wall of the cave. So the only thing the cave dwellers can see is this shadow play. They have been sitting in this position since they were born, so they think these shadows are all there are.

Imagine now that one of the cave dwellers manages to free himself from his bonds. The first thing he asks himself is where all these shadows on the cave wall come from. What do you think happens when he turns around and sees the figures being held up above the wall? To begin with he is dazzled by the sharp sunlight. He is also dazzled by the clarity of the figures because until now he has only seen their shadow. If he manages to climb over the wall and get past the fire into the world outside, he will be even more dazzled. But after rubbing his eyes he will be struck by the beauty of everything. For the first time he will see colors and clear shapes. He will see the real animals and flowers that the cave shadows were only poor reflections of. But even now he will ask himself where all the animals and flowers come from. Then he will see the sun in the sky, and realize that this is what gives life to these flowers and animals, just as the fire made the shadows visible.

The joyful cave dweller could now have gone skipping away into the countryside, delighting in his new-found freedom. But instead he thinks of all the others who are still down in the cave. He goes back. Once there, he tries to convince the cave dwellers that the shadows on the cave wall are but flickering reflections of 'real' things. But they don't believe him. They point to the cave wall and say that what they see is all there is. Finally they kill him.

What Plato was illustrating in the Myth of the Cave is

the philosopher's road from shadowy images to the true ideas behind all natural phenomena. He was probably also thinking of Socrates, whom the 'cave dwellers' killed because he disturbed their conventional ideas and tried to light the way to true insight. The Myth of the Cave illustrates Socrates' courage and his sense of pedagogic responsibility.

Plato's point was that the relationship between the darkness of the cave and the world beyond corresponds to the relationship between the forms of the natural world and the world of ideas. Not that he meant that the natural world is dark and dreary, but that it is dark and dreary *in comparison with* the clarity of ideas. A picture of a beautiful landscape is not dark and dreary either. But it is only a picture.

The Philosophic State
The Myth of the Cave is found in Plato's dialogue, the *Republic*. In this dialogue Plato also presents a picture of the 'ideal state,' that is to say an imaginary, ideal, or what we would call a Utopian, state. Briefly, we could say that Plato believed the state should be governed by philosophers. He bases his explanation of this on the construction of the human body.

According to Plato, the human body is composed of three parts: the head, the chest, and the abdomen. For each of these three parts there is a corresponding faculty of the soul. *Reason* belongs to the head, *will* belongs to the chest, and *appetite* belongs to the abdomen. Each of these soul faculties also has an ideal, or 'virtue.' Reason aspires to *wisdom*, 43

Will aspires to *courage*, and Appetite must be curbed so that *temperance* can be exercised. Only when the three parts of the body function together as a unity do we get a harmonious or 'virtuous' individual. At school, a child must first learn to curb its appetites, then it must develop courage, and finally reason leads to wisdom.

Plato now imagines a state built up exactly like the tripartite human body. Where the body has head, chest, and abdomen, the State has *rulers, auxiliaries,* and *laborers* (farmers, for example). Here Plato clearly uses Greek medical science as his model. Just as a healthy and harmonious man exercises balance and temperance, so a 'virtuous' state is characterized by everyone knowing their place in the overall picture.

Like every aspect of Plato's philosophy, his political philosophy is characterized by *rationalism*. The creation of a good state depends on its being governed with *reason*. Just as the head governs the body, so philosophers must rule society.

Let us attempt a simple illustration of the relationship between the three parts of man and the state:

BODY	SOUL	VIRTUE	STATE
head	reason	wisdom	rulers
chest	will	courage	auxiliaries
abdomen	appetite	temperance	laborers

Plato's ideal state is not unlike the old Hindu caste system, in which each and every person has his or her particular function for the good of the whole. Even before Plato's time the Hindu caste system had the same tripartite division between the auxiliary caste (or priest caste), the warrior caste, and the laborer caste. Nowadays we would perhaps call Plato's state totalitarian. But it is worth noting that he believed women could govern just as effectively as men for the simple reason that the rulers govern by virtue of their *reason*. Women, he asserted, have exactly the same powers of reasoning as men, provided they get the same training and are exempt from child rearing and housekeeping. In Plato's ideal state, rulers and warriors are not allowed family life or private property. The rearing of children is considered too important to be left to the individual and should be the responsibility of the state. (Plato was the first philosopher to advocate state-organized nursery schools and full-time education.)

After a number of significant political setbacks, Plato wrote the *Laws*, in which he described the 'constitutional state' as the next-best state. He now reintroduced both private property and family ties. Women's freedom thus became more restricted. However, he did say that a state that does not educate and train women is like a man who only trains his right arm.

All in all, we can say that Plato had a positive view of women – considering the time he lived in. In the dialogue *Symposium*, he gives a woman, the legendary priestess *Diotima*, the honor of having given Socrates his philosophic insight.

So that was Plato. His astonishing theories have been discussed – and criticized – for more than two thousand years. The first man to do so was one of the pupils from his own Academy. His name was Aristotle, and he was the third great philosopher from Athens.

ARISTOTLE

Philosopher and Scientist

You were probably astonished by Plato's theory of ideas. You are not the only one! I do not know whether you swallowed the whole thing – hook, line, and sinker – or whether you had any critical comments. But if you did have, you can be sure that the self-same criticism was raised by *Aristotle* (384–322 B.C.), who was a pupil at Plato's Academy for almost twenty years.

Aristotle was not a native of Athens. He was born in Macedonia and came to Plato's Academy when Plato was 61. Aristotle's father was a respected physician – and therefore a scientist. This background already tells us something about Aristotle's philosophic project. What he was most interested in was nature study. He was not only the last of the great Greek philosophers, he was Europe's first great biologist.

Taking it to extremes, we could say that Plato was so engrossed in his eternal forms, or 'ideas,' that he took very little notice of the changes in nature. Aristotle, on the other hand, was preoccupied with just these changes – or with what we nowadays describe as natural processes.

To exaggerate even more, we could say that Plato turned his back on the sensory world and shut his eyes to everything we see around us. (He wanted to escape from the cave and look out over the eternal world of ideas!) Aristotle did the opposite: he got down on all fours and studied frogs and fish, anemones and poppies.

While Plato used his reason, Aristotle used his senses as well.

We find decisive differences between the two, not least in their writing. Plato was a poet and mythologist; Aristotle's writings were as dry and precise as an encyclopedia. On the other hand, much of what he wrote was based on up-to-the-minute field studies.

Records from antiquity refer to 170 titles supposedly written by Aristotle. Of these, 47 are preserved. These are not complete books; they consist largely of lecture notes. In his time, philosophy was still mainly an oral activity.

The significance of Aristotle in European culture is due not least to the fact that he created the terminology that scientists use today. He was the great organizer who founded and classified the various sciences.

Since Aristotle wrote on all the sciences, I will limit myself to some of the most important areas. Now that I have told you such a lot about Plato, you must start by hearing how Aristotle refuted Plato's theory of ideas. Later we will look at the way he formulated his own natural philosophy, since it was Aristotle who summed up what the natural philosophers before him had said. We'll see how he categorizes our concepts and founds the discipline of Logic as a science.

And finally I'll tell you a little about Aristotle's view of man and society.

No Innate Ideas

Like the philosophers before him, Plato wanted to find the eternal and immutable in the midst of all change. So he found the perfect ideas that were superior to the sensory world. Plato furthermore held that ideas were more real than all the phenomena of nature. First came the idea 'horse,' then came all the sensory world's horses trotting along like shadows on a cave wall. The idea 'chicken' came before both the chicken and the egg.

Aristotle thought Plato had turned the whole thing upside down. He agreed with his teacher that the particular horse 'flows' and that no horse lives forever. He also agreed that the actual form of the horse is eternal and immutable. But the 'idea' horse was simply a concept that we humans had formed *after* seeing a certain number of horses. The 'idea' or 'form' horse thus had no existence of its own. To Aristotle, the 'idea' or the 'form' horse was made up of the horse's characteristics – which define what we today call the horse *species*.

To be more precise: by 'form' horse, Aristotle meant that which is common to all horses. And here the metaphor of the gingerbread mold does not hold up because the mold exists independently of the particular gingerbread cookies. Aristotle did not believe in the existence of any such molds or forms that, as it were, lay on their own shelf beyond the natural world. On the contrary, to Aristotle the 'forms' were *in the things*, because they were the particular characteristics of these things.

So Aristotle disagreed with Plato that the 'idea' chicken came before the chicken. What Aristotle called the 'form' chicken is present in every single chicken as the chicken's particular set characteristics – for one, that it lays eggs. The real chicken and the 'form' chicken are thus just as inseparable as body and soul.

And that is really the essence of Aristotle's criticism of Plato's theory of ideas. But you should not ignore the fact that this was a dramatic turn of thought. The highest degree of reality, in Plato's theory, was that which we *think* with our reason. It was equally apparent to Aristotle that the highest degree of reality is that which we *perceive* with our senses. Plato thought that all the things we see in the natural world were purely reflections of things that existed in the higher reality of the world of ideas – and thereby in the human soul. Aristotle thought the opposite: things that are in the human soul were purely reflections of natural objects. So nature is the real world. According to Aristotle, Plato was trapped in a mythical world picture in which the human imagination was confused with the real world.

Aristotle pointed out that nothing exists in consciousness that has not first been experienced by the senses. Plato would have said that there is nothing in the natural world that has not first existed in the world of ideas. Aristotle held that Plato was thus 'doubling the number of things.' He explained a horse by referring to the 'idea' horse. But what kind of an explanation is that? Where does the 'idea' horse come from, is my question. Might there not even be 49 a third horse, which the 'idea' horse is just an imitation of?

Aristotle held that all our thoughts and ideas have come into our consciousness through what we have heard and seen. But we also have an innate power of reason. We have no innate ideas, as Plato held, but we have the innate faculty of organizing all sensory impressions into categories and classes. This is how concepts such as 'stone,' 'plant,' 'animal,' and 'human' arise. Similarly there arise concepts like 'horse,' 'lobster,' and 'canary.'

Aristotle did not deny that humans have innate reason. On the contrary, it is precisely *reason*, according to Aristotle, that is man's most distinguishing characteristic. But our reason is completely empty until we have sensed something. So man has no innate 'ideas.'

The Form of a Thing Is Its Specific Characteristics

Having come to terms with Plato's theory of ideas, Aristotle decided that reality consisted of various separate things that constitute a unity of *form* and *substance*. The 'substance' is what things are made of, while the 'form' is each thing's specific characteristics.

A chicken is fluttering about in front of you. The chicken's 'form' is precisely that it flutters – and that it cackles and lays eggs. So by the 'form' of a chicken, we mean the specific characteristics of its species – or in other words, what it *does*. When the chicken dies – and cackles no more – its 'form' ceases to exist. The only thing that remains is the chicken's 'substance', but then it is no longer a chicken.

As I said earlier, Aristotle was concerned with the changes

in nature. 'Substance' always contains the potentiality to realize a specific 'form.' We could say that 'substance' always strives towards achieving an innate potentiality. Every change in nature, according to Aristotle, is a transformation of substance from the 'potential' to the 'actual.'

Yes, I'll explain what I mean. See if this funny story helps you. A sculptor is working on a large block of granite. He hacks away at the formless block every day. One day a little boy comes by and says, 'What are you looking for?' 'Wait and see,' answers the sculptor. After a few days the little boy comes back, and now the sculptor has carved a beautiful horse out of the granite. The boy stares at it in amazement, then he turns to the sculptor and says, 'How did you know it was in there?'

How indeed! In a sense, the sculptor had seen the horse's form in the block of granite, because that particular block of granite had the potentiality to be formed into the shape of a horse. Similarly Aristotle believed that everything in nature has the potentiality of realizing, or achieving, a specific 'form.'

Let us return to the chicken and the egg. A chicken's egg has the potentiality to become a chicken. This does not mean that all chicken's eggs become chickens – many of them end up on the breakfast table as fried eggs, omelettes, or scrambled eggs, without ever having realized their potentiality. But it is equally obvious that a chicken's egg cannot become a goose. *That* potentiality is not within a chicken's egg. The 'form' of a thing, then, says something about its limitation as well as its potentiality.

When Aristotle talks about the 'substance' and 'form' of

things, he does not only refer to living organisms. Just as it is the chicken's 'form' to cackle, flutter its wings, and lay eggs, it is the form of the stone to fall to the ground. Just as the chicken cannot help cackling, the stone cannot help falling to the ground. You can, of course, lift a stone and hurl it high into the air, but because it is the stone's nature to fall to the ground, you cannot hurl it to the moon. (Take care when you perform this experiment, because the stone might take revenge and find the shortest route back to the earth!)

The Final Cause

Before we leave the subject of all living and dead things having a 'form' that says something about their potential 'action,' I must add that Aristotle had a remarkable view of causality in nature.

Today when we talk about the 'cause' of anything, we mean *how* it came to happen. The windowpane was smashed because Peter hurled a stone through it; a shoe is made because the shoemaker sews pieces of leather together. But Aristotle held that there were different types of cause in nature. Altogether he named four different causes. It is important to understand what he meant by what he called the 'final cause.'

In the case of window smashing, it is quite reasonable to ask *why* Peter threw the stone. We are thus asking what his purpose was. There can be no doubt that purpose played a role, also, in the matter of the shoe being made. But Aristotle also took into account a similar 'purpose' when considering the purely lifeless processes in nature. Here's an example:

Why does it rain? You have probably learned that it rains because the moisture in the clouds cools and condenses into raindrops that are drawn to the earth by the force of gravity. Aristotle would have nodded in agreement. But he would have added that so far you have only mentioned three of the causes. The 'material cause' is that the moisture (the clouds) was there at the precise moment when the air cooled. The 'efficient cause' is that the moisture cools, and the 'formal cause' is that the 'form,' or nature of the water, is to fall to the earth. But if you stopped there, Aristotle would add that it rains *because* plants and animals need rainwater in order to grow. This he called the 'final cause.' Aristotle assigns the raindrops a life-task, or 'purpose.'

We would probably turn the whole thing upside down and say that plants grow because they find moisture. You can see the difference, can't you? Aristotle believed that there is a purpose behind everything in nature. It rains so that plants can grow; oranges and grapes grow so that people can eat them.

That is not the nature of scientific reasoning today. We say that food and water are necessary conditions of life for man and beast. Had we not had these conditions we would not have existed. But it is not the *purpose* of water or oranges to be food for us.

In the question of causality then, we are tempted to say that Aristotle was wrong. But let us not be too hasty. Many people believe that God created the world as it is so that all His creatures could live in it. Viewed in this way, it can naturally be claimed that there is water in the rivers because animals and humans need water to live. But now we are 53 talking about *God's* purpose. The raindrops and the waters of the river have no interest in our welfare.

Logic

The distinction between 'form' and 'substance' plays an important part in Aristotle's explanation of the way we discern things in the world.

When we discern things, we classify them in various groups or categories. I see a horse, then I see another horse, and another. The horses are not exactly alike, but they have something in common, and this common something is the horse's 'form.' Whatever might be distinctive, or individual, belongs to the horse's 'substance.'

So we go around pigeonholing everything. We put cows in cowsheds, horses in stables, pigs in pigsties, and chickens in chicken coops. Notice that we do the same thing in our minds. We distinguish between things made of stone, things made of wool, and things made of rubber. We distinguish between things that are alive or dead, and we distinguish between vegetable, animal, and human.

Aristotle wanted to do a thorough clearing up in nature's 'room.' He tried to show that everything in nature belongs to different categories and subcategories.

Go into your room. Pick up something, anything, from the floor. Whatever you take, you will find that what you are holding belongs to a higher category. The day you see something you are unable to classify you will get a shock. If, for example, you discover a small whatsit, and you can't really say whether it is animal, vegetable, or mineral – I don't think you would dare touch it.

Saying animal, vegetable, and mineral reminds me of that party game where the victim is sent outside the room, and when he comes in again he has to guess what everyone else is thinking of. Everyone has agreed to think of Fluffy, the cat, which at the moment is in the neighbor's garden. The victim comes in and begins to guess. The others must only answer 'yes' or 'no.' If the victim is a good Aristotelian – and therefore no victim – the game could go pretty much as follows:

Is it concrete? (Yes!) Mineral? (No!) Is it alive? (Yes!) Vegetable? (No!) Animal? (Yes!) Is it a bird? (No!) Is it a mammal? (Yes!) Is it the whole animal? (Yes!) Is it a cat? (Yes!) Is it Fluffy? (Yeah! Laughter . . .)

So Aristotle invented that game. We ought to give Plato the credit for having invented hide-and-seek. Democritus has already been credited with having invented Lego.

Aristotle was a meticulous organizer who set out to clarify our concepts. In fact, he founded the science of *Logic*. He demonstrated a number of laws governing conclusions or proofs that were valid. One example will suffice. If I first establish that 'all living creatures are mortal' (first premise), and then establish that a 'dog is a living creature' (second premise), I can then elegantly conclude that 'a dog is mortal.'

The example demonstrates that Aristotle's logic was based on the correlation of terms, in this case 'living creature' and 'mortal.' Even though one has to admit that the above conclusion is 100% valid, we may also add that it hardly tells us anything new. We already knew that a dog was 'mortal.' (He is a 'dog' and all dogs are 'living creatures' – which are 'mortal,' unlike the rock of Mount 55

Everest.) Certainly we knew that. But the relationship between classes of things is not always so obvious. From time to time it can be necessary to clarify our concepts.

For example: Is it really possible that tiny little baby mice suckle just like lambs and piglets? Mice certainly do not lay eggs (When did I last see a mouse's egg?). So they give birth to live young – just like pigs and sheep. But we call animals that bear live young mammals – and mammals are animals that feed on their mother's milk. So – we got there. We had the answer inside us but we had to think it through. We forgot for the moment that mice really do suckle from their mother. Perhaps it was because we have never seen a baby mouse being suckled, for the simple reason that mice are rather shy of humans when they suckle their young.

Nature's Scale

When Aristotle 'clears up' in life, he first of all points out that everything in the natural world can be divided into two main categories. On the one hand there are *nonliving things*, such as stones, drops of water, or clumps of soil. These things have no potentiality for change. According to Aristotle, nonliving things can only change through external influence. Only *living things* have the potentiality for change.

Aristotle divides 'living things' into two different categories. One comprises *plants*, and the other *creatures*. Finally, these 'creatures' can also be divided into two subcategories, namely *animals* and *humans*.

You have to admit that Aristotle's categories are clear and simple. There is a decisive difference between a living and a nonliving thing, for example a rose and a stone, just as there is a decisive difference between a plant and an animal, for example a rose and a horse. I would also claim that there definitely is a difference between a horse and a man. But what exactly does this difference consist of?

When Aristotle divides natural phenomena into various categories, his criterion is the object's characteristics, or more specifically what it *can do* or what it *does*.

All living things (plants, animals, humans) have the ability to absorb nourishment, to grow, and to propagate. All 'living creatures' (animals and humans) have in addition the ability to perceive the world around them and to move about. Moreover, all humans have the ability to think – or otherwise to order their perceptions into various categories and classes.

So there are in reality no sharp boundaries in the natural world. We observe a gradual transition from simple growths to more complicated plants, from simple animals to more complicated animals. At the top of this 'scale' is man – who according to Aristotle lives the whole life of nature. Man grows and absorbs nourishment like plants, he has feelings and the ability to move like animals, but he also has a specific characteristic peculiar to humans, and that is the ability to think rationally.

Therefore, man has a spark of divine reason. Yes, I did say divine. From time to time Aristotle reminds us that there must be a God who started all movement in the natural world. Therefore God must be at the very top of nature's scale.

Aristotle imagined the movement of the stars and the

planets guiding all movement on Earth. But there had to be something causing the heavenly bodies to move. Aristotle called this the 'first mover,' or 'God.' The 'first mover' is itself at rest, but it is the 'formal cause' of the movement of the heavenly bodies, and thus of all movement in nature.

Ethics

Let us go back to man. According to Aristotle, man's 'form' comprises a soul, which has a plant-like part, an animal part, and a rational part. And now he asks: how should we live? What does it require to live a good life? His answer: Man can only achieve happiness by using all his abilities and capabilities.

Aristotle held that there are three forms of happiness. The first form of happiness is a life of pleasure and enjoyment. The second form of happiness is a life as a free and responsible citizen. The third form of happiness is a life as thinker and philosopher.

Aristotle then emphasized that all three criteria must be present at the same time for man to find happiness and fulfilment. He rejected all forms of imbalance. Had he lived today he might have said that a person who only develops his body lives a life that is just as unbalanced as someone who only uses his head. Both extremes are an expression of a warped way of life.

The same applies in human relationships, where Aristotle advocated the 'Golden Mean.' We must be neither cowardly nor rash, but courageous (too little courage is cowardice, too much is rashness), neither miserly nor extravagant but
liberal (not liberal enough is miserly, too liberal is

extravagant). The same goes for eating. It is dangerous to eat too little, but also dangerous to eat too much. The ethics of both Plato and Aristotle contain echoes of Greek medicine: only by exercising balance and temperance will I achieve a happy or 'harmonious' life.

Politics

The undesirability of cultivating extremes is also expressed in Aristotle's view of society. He says that man is by nature a 'political animal.' Without a society around us, we are not real people, he claimed. He pointed out that the family and the village satisfy our primary needs of food, warmth, marriage, and child rearing. But the highest form of human fellowship is only to be found in the state.

This leads to the question of how the state should be organized. (You remember Plato's 'philosophic state'?) Aristotle describes three good forms of constitution.

One is *monarchy*, or kingship – which means there is only one head of state. For this type of constitution to be good, it must not degenerate into 'tyranny' – that is, when one ruler governs the state to his own advantage. Another good form of constitution is *aristocracy*, in which there is a larger or smaller group of rulers. This constitutional form must beware of degenerating into an 'oligarchy' – when the government is run by a few people. An example of that would be a junta. The third good constitutional form is what Aristotle called *polity*, which means democracy. But this form also has its negative aspect. A democracy can quickly develop into mob rule. (Even if the tyrannic Hitler had not become head of state in Germany, all the lesser

Nazis could have formed a terrifying mob rule.)

Views on Women

Finally, let us look at Aristotle's views on women. His were unfortunately not as uplifting as Plato's. Aristotle was more inclined to believe that women were incomplete in some way. A woman was an 'unfinished man.' In reproduction, woman is passive and receptive whilst man is active and productive; for the child inherits only the male characteristics, claimed Aristotle. He believed that all the child's characteristics lay complete in the male sperm. The woman was the soil, receiving and bringing forth the seed, whilst the man was the 'sower.' Or, in Aristotelian language, the man provides the 'form' and the woman contributes the 'substance.'

It is of course both astonishing and highly regrettable that an otherwise so intelligent man could be so wrong about the relationship of the sexes. But it demonstrates two things: first, that Aristotle could not have had much practical experience regarding the lives of women and children, and second, it shows how wrong things can go when men are allowed to reign supreme in the fields of philosophy and science.

Aristotle's erroneous view of the sexes was doubly harmful because it was his – rather than Plato's – view that held sway throughout the Middle Ages. The church thus inherited a view of women that is entirely without foundation in the Bible. Jesus was certainly no woman hater!